Everyone is Reading

Juliet Partridge

Illustrated by Kim Gamble

Everyone is Reading

Mark is reading a plan
to make a model plane.

Jan is reading her favourite book,
over and over again.

Gran is reading a postcard
that Cousin Billy wrote.

Pop is reading a catalogue
to choose his winter coat.

Dad is reading a recipe
to make some bread for tea.

Claire is reading the paper
to see what's on TV.

Everyone is reading, except for little Tim.
He is lying in his bed.

Who will read to him?

Everyone is Busy

Pop is in the greenhouse,
watering his plants.

Tim is in the flowerbed,
digging down to France.

Jan is in the sandpit,
using her new rake.

Claire is on the front lawn,
stretching like a snake.

Gran is planting roses,
kneeling on the mat.

Dad is playing cricket,
using his new bat.

Everyone is busy,
but Mark has lost his plane.

Who will help him find it
before it starts to rain?

Everyone is Doing Maths

Jan is pouring sand
into the tallest tin.

Tim is racing snails
to see which one will win.

Mark is counting coins
to buy another plane.

Dad is weighing flour
to make some bread again.

Gran is matching patterns
to finish off her quilt.

Pop is looking pleased with
the kennel he's just built.

Now it's nearly lunchtime
and the table must be set,
but Claire is doing her jigsaw
and she hasn't finished yet!